Deafening Silence

ALIYA SIDDIQUI

BLUEROSE PUBLISHERS
India | U.K.

Copyright © Aliya Siddiqui 2024

All rights reserved by author. No part of this publication may be reproduced, stored in a retrieval system or transmitted in any form or by any means, electronic, mechanical, photocopying, recording or otherwise, without the prior permission of the author. Although every precaution has been taken to verify the accuracy of the information contained herein, the publisher assumes no responsibility for any errors or omissions. No liability is assumed for damages that may result from the use of information contained within.

BlueRose Publishers takes no responsibility for any damages, losses, or liabilities that may arise from the use or misuse of the information, products, or services provided in this publication.

For permissions requests or inquiries regarding this publication, please contact:

BLUEROSE PUBLISHERS
www.BlueRoseONE.com
info@bluerosepublishers.com
+91 8882 898 898
+4407342408967

ISBN: 978-93-6452-034-8

Cover Design: Sadhna Kumari
Typesetting: Pooja Sharma

First Edition: December 2024

Dedication

To my childhood

About Author

Aliya Siddiqui, born on November 21, 2005, has lived a life deeply intertwined with words and emotions. From her earliest years, she was captivated by the art of storytelling and poetry, influenced by the presence of her grandfather, Syed Iqbal Hussain, a poet whose words left an indelible mark on her soul. Those tender years spent with him are among her most cherished memories, filled with inspiration, warmth, and an ever-present sense of wonder. Yet, it was the nightly stories read by her mother that truly ignited her passion. Her mother, with her books and bedtime tales, nurtured Aliya's imagination, helping her escape into the vast, magical worlds that lay between the pages. Amidst this creative nurturing, Aliya's father played a crucial role, encouraging her to keep writing and constantly motivating her to take her craft seriously. He was the one who told her that her words mattered and urged her to one day share them with the world.

Writing soon became more than just a pastime; it was her sanctuary. In moments when life felt suffocating, when the weight of the world pressed down on her, Aliya found refuge in her words. Writing became her breath, her release—a way to pour out her pain, fear, and hope onto paper. It was in these moments of vulnerability that Aliya felt most alive, as if she was finally hearing the sound of her own voice amidst the noise of the world.

Though she kept her words to herself for years, the quiet power of her poetry eventually caught the attention of those close to her. Friends, touched by her raw honesty and emotional depth, urged her to share her gift with the world. Now, Aliya is stepping into the light, ready to publish her debut poetry collection—a deeply personal exploration of suffering, pain, and healing.

Though she had initially kept her writings private, the encouragement of friends motivated her to consider publishing her work. Today, Aliya is not only working on her debut poetry collection but also exploring new projects, including novels centered around thrillers, mysteries, and murder mysteries. Her writing, a blend of emotional depth and suspense, marks the beginning of what promises to be a compelling literary journey.

The wounds were just healing and I found them getting stabbed again, maybe this time I won't draw out the dagger, to never forget the taste of torment.

Contents

Torture and tranquility *1*

To be a poetry? *2*

Mere lies *3*

A token of farewell *4*

A hidden door *5*

Everything has a story *6*

Who's the villain *7*

A burial ground *8*

Is love violent? *9*

Adorned territories *10*

Melancholic nights *12*

Her doe eyes or town of memories *13*

Nostalgia was never a friend *14*

A heart an abyss *15*

A childhood utopia or a betrayal? *18*

Diary with surprise *19*

Barren language *20*

Scars that always bleed *23*

Beauty with flaws *25*

A childhood utopia or a betrayal? 32

Hour of separation 34

A dagger of lies 35

A poet's tradegy 36

At last 37

What suffice between the end 39

Frozen town 49

An hourglass of torment 50

Torture and tranquility

I have been writing between torture and tranquility,
Some days the pages of my journal bleeds in murk,
and often the torment inside the head was so dreadful
but writing it down was never a desire,
as if I want it to stay undefined to me.

Some days the words were drenched in the rain of tears
as no longer the heart could cage the clouds of Agony.

And Some days the pages breathe the fragrance of bliss and hope as if the happiness was fluttering from the heart and the vibrant colours of life inside the head concealed the echos of Agony, and I wanted to inhale all of it. Some days it showered in the warmth of love and ecstasy that melted all
the torment.

- Aliya Siddiqui

To be a poetry?

Never I yearn to be turned into a poetry, such a splendour it seems for those whom verses are written for, but as well what a shrouded terror it can carry?

-Aliya Siddiqui

Mere lies

They call it mere lies...

Those words you served to my heart, burnt it to ever be wrenched in gore by your lies again.
Oh lies, mere lies I am indebted of this favor to murder my heartbeats which once believed.

- Aliya Siddiqui

A token of farewell

When I am dead all my poetries belong to you as a token of farewell from this world,

My soul never belonged to this world, so do my heart, but isn't it tragic when all my words and poems were the rhythm of this beating heart, would no longer beat but still the rhyme of every seasons my heart lived in, will be stored in my diaries.

And in the end what is it, to even name yours and belong to you when no longer your own words could be declaimed in your voice?

-Aliya Siddiqui

A hidden door

When some doors open up a chapter in your life,
Where even the language is so obscure that turning the pages further feels impossible,
Suddenly, there's a gust of fragrance,
Carrying nostalgia between the pages.

Is this nostalgia a crippling emotion to be buried,
As this heart is incapable of bearing it
Or a blissful token, uncovering the curtains of torment,
Inviting you to embrace it and again let this heart ignite
in the warmth which you nearly buried.

-Aliya Siddiqui

Everything has a story

When I heard that everything has a story, all i could wonder were the buried stories of a child under the shadows of cruelty,

How the walls of coldness and gloomy memories concealed the enchanted ecstasy of childhood nearly choking them to death, even no oceans of tears could ever wash away those walls, no thundering screams inside could Crack them to breath again.

Despite all this enigma trapping me between the black and white contrast of memories, a hope forged open a window to the midst of my heart,once more instilling it with the bliss and ecstasy when nearly i saw all those stories slipping into an abyss.

Who's the villain

In the darkest nights she shoved her shattered self in the abyss,

Standing in the most scarlet shades of maroon, sealing the gateway of that gorge with her hands dyed in the blood of her ruptured heart.

Yet Did locking herself conced the verity of being the villain of own life or to find some pastel warmth, that caged persona burnt itself in the cold darkness as an apology to oneself?

A burial ground

Would you entitle poetry to be chained by hypocrisy or kissed by sincerity?

When we writers say poetry keep us alive but at same it's the burial ground of us.

-Aliya Siddiqui

Is love violent?

All I have heard of Love is that, it's solacing and exalted, where the heart is crowned by the majestic and golorious stories inscribed in the sapphires of the diadem.

But Have they forgotten to mention How violent act it is ? As the hands which crowned the heart were coloured in the blood of same shabby dripping heart.

-Aliya Siddiqui

Adorned territories

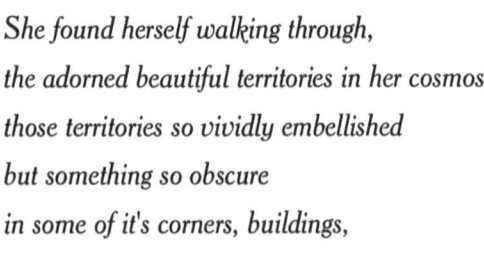

She found herself walking through,
the adorned beautiful territories in her cosmos,
those territories so vividly embellished
but something so obscure
in some of it's corners, buildings,
roads, and countrysides.

A strange quiver ran through her body
at the conviction of what this enchanting adornment is.
And a deafening silence seized the entire existence to only let her heartbeats echo everywhere at the discerning truth of those territories embellished with the gems and pearls of poetry, literature, and verses.

Still Obscure? No,
it was all a gloomy land immortalized by suffering and torment crafted into words and songs scripted,
painted into lavish paintings on the walls of abandoned buildings and palaces.
Did she just let it go unheeded or didn't paint the museum of pain and torture, painting it with the brightest shades,
trying to conceal something?
Or the truth of this entire territory, so to never abandon it and again name it a gloomy land as it was.

Maybe a day will rise to walk away from her adorned territories and palace to a blissful cottage where heavenly mornings stir into starry elysian evenings, but the echos of her words and some parts of her still remain, narrating the stories as however the new eyes may discern looking on those walls and buildings.

-Aliya Siddiqui

Melancholic nights

Melancholy was so murderous on some nights
That closing my eyes became a nightmare,
And agony was trapped so deep in my lungs,
I could barely inhale.
At least the tears flooded the path of my screams,
When echoes of words ripped open my heart.

My mind was no less than a torture cell,
Tangling me in memories,
Playing those echoes of words on repeat,
Ripping me open again and again.

Did my heart become the victim of my mind in all this torment,
Or were those words a poison to my mind,
Ripping open my heart?

-Aliya Siddiqui

Her doe eyes or town of memories

Eyes, doe eyes, her gleaming eyes smiled, gazing at the majestic, vivid sky.
Perhaps those eyes spoke more than words ever could, from then until now.
And now, an utterly cold, icy town resides within them,
Memories of childhood buried beneath layers of snow,
Frosting the lake of tears.

What shall we say to these eyes?
What are you? A terror of silver beauty,
Wearing a crown of crystal tears,
Or a cold soul, waiting somewhere for the blizzard to end?
                                                    -Aliya Siddiqui

Nostalgia was never a friend

Maybe Nostalgia was never a friend.
Even if its a reminiscence of everything I have ever loved,
I want it to be blurred enough in my memories,
to ever get my eyes blurred with the tears of memories.
But this mind has build a house of memories,
which can never be devoid of this taste of Nostalgia.
Can't this nostalgia rain out with my tears once and for all?

A heart an abyss

Is my heart an abyss of the wounds you have bestowed onto it?
No matter how murderous they were,
it swallowed all of them, feeding it on that one illusion that it was the last of all.

-Aliya Siddiqui

Cherishing some people, the moments you share with them, are like inhaling an aroma too abiding to ever be replaced, the soul is blossomed with the fragrance of amuse. Their presence put on the most radiant smile on your face to ever be seen.

And there comes a day where all of it starts drifting to Memories, where your heart beating in all the rhymes to live those moments again. Now cherishing those back in mind with tears in eyes.

Does Pieces of reminiscing moments becomes a home or is it a longing for home?

-Aliya Siddiqui

The dried tears between the words while writing,
were just the mere reflections of wounds
that never bleeds, but once were lethargic.

-Aliya Siddiqui

A childhood utopia or a betrayal?

The utopian vision which once was blossomed in childhood, shattered into pieces just in a jiff,

When the shadows of cruelty and reality hit her doe eyes, than all she knew was a dystopic insight,

but still she hopes for just a pinch of Utopia.

-Aliya Siddiqui

Diary with surprise

A decade this diary retained inside the cabinet unseen,
although its glimpse was ample for nexus of words.

A decade it persisted untouched, while the grasp in hand was
enough to prompt Meraki,

A decade elapsed without writing, when the ink filled the blank
pages into frisky hopes

A decade after it unlocked, weirdly eyes falls on a dried roses
between the pages holding fragrance of self love and memories.

-Aliya Siddiqui

Barren language

*There is a language so barren
which lack words, sometimes it's a lump in throat
choking the words, only tears make their way out
as if the voice is devoured by nullity.*

*The enigma inside is so murky,
that cripple the ribs to stifle
until the breathes begin to smother*

*And the swallowed screams were so thundering
that it emerged the storms inside.*

All I knew was, 'nothing could be more torturing than my own mind,'

but also in some corner of this chaotic mind,
there was a flower blooming and fluttering
the fragrance of hope, love and every tranquil emotions
I ever felt and knew,

as if I treasured a pinch of each of these emotions
in that corner in a bud and let it bloom in some of the darkest times.

- Aliya Siddiqui

A Writer's masterpiece delight others out there, unaware of the trivial truth, that masterpiece was fashioned by the shattered pieces of their soul.

-Aliya Siddiqui

Scars that always bleed

I wonder if the scars on heart could ever be entirely eclipsed by love, if shattered pieces could ever be held together, I can't say about love but Hope has always been a warmth to heart even if it was dripping in blood.

- Aliya Siddiqui

The dried tears between

the words while writing, were just the mere reflections of wounds that never bleeds, but once were lethargic.

- Aliya Siddiqui

Beauty with flaws

I sit at the window at night, look at the moon hiding in the willows.

There I find the,' Art of Kintsugi'. Moon embracing the flaws bestowed, by the willows Giving, a sensation of Beauty with Flaws.

- Aliya Siddiqui

Sometimes I feel like words from my diary and notes

may vanish when I am gone, as I would never want one to know, "What a disaster and abyss of catastrophe my mind was when I was trying to disappear but couldn't, when trembling fingers froze to even hold the pen anymore.

I wonder How did the paper handle it and How insane could it be to even write out of your crippled self, which when were meant to be screams not words."

- Aliya Siddiqui

I wonder if it's a favor or a curse for writers to feel everything too deeply. If our mind is chaos, then what would the heart look like? Maybe a blood dripping materpiece to bleed on paper.

- Aliya Siddiqui

Maybe I can mask the Agony behind my silence, maybe some words may never be spoken, as those are ruthlessly stabbed by my own hands and now the silence is ripping me apart.

- Aliya Siddiqui

When I heard Anne Frank said,

"Paper has more patience than people,"

since that day the pages of diary became my ideal listeners, the ink on those pages let out the veracity, the drops of tears on those pages between the words were the little glimpse of tornadoes of chaos, I had inside me.

- Aliya Siddiqui

Paper beared more emotions, more tears, ,more untold things, plenty of reactions in the form of words.

- Aliya Siddiqui

I wonder if reminiscent could ever be free from torment or if no ecstasy could ever conceal the hidden turmoils in mind?

- Aliya Siddiqui

A childhood utopia or a betrayal?

The utopian vision which once was blossomed in childhood, shattered into pieces just in a jiff,

when the shadows of cruelty and reality hit her doe eyes, than all she knew was a dystopic sight, but still she hopes for just a pinch of Utopia.

- Aliya Siddiqui

When I looked back into the words
written a decade ago in my diaries.
I found it like, a child was running in the meadows of serenity and her eyes gleamed at every flower she looked at, and every colours she touched painted her mind with fantasies.

But little did she know was,
those one day would turn into an island of Agony,
the flowers once she looked at would perish in heat of hatred and the vivid colours which painter her mind would freeze in black and white,
to mask all the fantasies.

-Aliya Siddiqui

Hour of separation

"You never know the warmth of love until the hour of separation."

When you no longer see those eyes which has always been the oceans of comfort.

When no longer memories are a relief, it's a torment knocking in your mind.

When an unknown fear chokes you to even breathe.

When you come to an edge where all you question is, " Was that warmth to ignite everything or burn it into ashes?"

A dagger of lies

When you held the dagger dipped in the nectar of lies at my back whispering the words of myth in my ears,

seemed as if those lies eclipsed my heart entirely, so I whispered back,

placing the dagger at my throat, "better you shove this dagger down my throat looking into my eyes, i only yearn that you pour the truth in my heart, maybe than that won't be a wistful death for me."

- Aliya Siddiqui

A poet's tradegy

I say Poets are a mere tragedy,

When write about the aching heart it's glorified as poetry.

Not many discern those words are the graves of pain and grieve, What stabs me more is, my own hand burying it all with an enigmatic smile, realizing THE SCARS..

Those aren't just scars but Monsters given birth on the funeral of feelings.

Monsters inscribed within the layers of memories, haunting me reciting my own memory and words as if I was the villain of my ownself who kept burying the pain which never died.

- Aliya Siddiqui

At last

Why is death always talked as something haunting and wistful, but it's just a mere truth. If something is haunting than it's when Death knocks your door, and all that was to be found inside was already lost before it's arrival.

I wonder wouldn't death be piteous this time to find an utterly devoured soul and a raptured heart? The same soul rejoins, " Call me Morbid but A thousand times I have fallen in the abyss of end and still existed, now's the time but I couldn't draw a line to self slaughtering to wait for this moment."

- Aliya Siddiqui

"You spoke of me as a blackhole in your story, how wicked of your words which eclipsed my back story that, 'merely I was a dying star' in that cosmos,

in which your tale was creating galaxies

while burying the antecedents in my own

core, while I turned into realm of grief you wrote me as Villain in this story, and the exquisite tradegy of this story is I can't engulf you, as you were the wicked Author of this entire tale."
All I question now is, still Am I wicked or you?

- Aliya Siddiqui

What suffice between the end

How can being morbid more excruciating than self destruction,
when everyday you wake up with a soul
so empty, yet a mind full of turmoil,
each moment is stuck in the hour glass of torment
leaving you in the midst of stifled breathes.
The echoes in your head begin to devour you into someone that you no longer can recognize,
Being morbid is a final visit of death to you,
embracing you as such every breathe is smothered inside,

but than does self destruction either suffice between being dead and alive
or is it a your own created hell inside the head devouring every part of you?

- Aliya Siddiqui

Isn't my tangled breath enough to obscures the Agony or is it the Agony filling up my lungs to collapse?

- Aliya Siddiqui

Won't it be more murderous when you start finding a way out of the coldness in your heart, when you begin unwrapping the layers of frozen torment and it melts through your tears to burndown the aching cold, enfolding you in the warmth disgused in a betrayal again?

- Aliya Siddiqui

Once the things which were the warmth to my heart, turned it too cold to ever be ignited again, but still that piercing coldness couldn't froze those memories beating inside my heart.

Maybe you would never know,
How you turned this heart of mine
into a graveyard of words,
and a home of wounds that you bestowed
on it as a present of my love.

If I could ever talk to time,
I would ask will this shattered heart of mine ever be
held together again or will it drown in it's own blood
in the hour glass of time.

- Aliya Siddiqui

The darkest shades of blood becomes the most scarlet adornment of poetry.

- Aliya Siddiqui

Did those words written on paper just mask the screams of Agony or did those words turn into the graves of screams?

- Aliya Siddiqui

Memories are beautiful catastrophe,
that holds me between black and white,
when I dwell deep into it the pain
no longer is by masked anything.
The torment never ends in it.
Neither I ever wanna erase it
nor reminisce it as those were
once the moments I cherished.

- Aliya Siddiqui

The nights when my mind is a room full of catastrophes, seems as if the thoughts suffocate every micro corners of it, to find an escape into my lungs as a poison smothering my breathes and dyeing my blood in darker shade,

every moment when the valves of my mind seemed closed and obscured by the mask of agony.

Is this mask of Agony a poison to murder every breathe inside me or is this murderous venom too dispersed in my blood to even perceive if it's poison all that i could draw in?

- Aliya Siddiqui

Frozen town

Even the air around is icing over now,
seems like the blood in my veins is turning
into the frozen crystal of rubies,
as if this heart of mine only know
the season of gloomy winters,

A canopy of murky smog forging
the sequels of agonies into my heart,
to even know if my heart still beats
in the seasons of spring.

And even if any tenderness
uncovers this murky smog...,
I can't say if the warmth could,
ever touch the edges of my heart
but rather will perish it as that's all,
I have known either a piecercing coldness
or a violent flare burning everything down.

In the end All I shall ask to myself, "Did my heart ever tasted a trivial sense of justice between all these battles of icy storms and violent flare blazes?"

An hourglass of torment

In the darkest nights,
her mind plans her own resurrection in the
most catastrophic ways.
It seize every valve of her mind to escape this torturing torment,
neither let the tears cast their way down through her eyes.
All she knows are, the empty eyes looking
at the hour glass and waiting for the dawn,
All again to be just haunted by the memories of adversities,
Bestowed on the chaste soul by a poisoned
mind every night.
As soon as it's dusk the soul cried, Oh my dear, Mercy!
A voice echos in every corner of her mind,
"You have had a thousand funerals in your mind, Why Am I to hold you together once again when all you do poison your mind mercilessly?"

- Aliya Siddiqui

www.ingramcontent.com/pod-product-compliance
Lightning Source LLC
LaVergne TN
LVHW041635070526
838199LV00052B/3382